Conservation of Energy

Suzanne Barchers

Consultant

Brent Tanner
Mechanical Engineer

Publishing Credits

Rachelle Cracchiolo, M.S.Ed., *Publisher*
Conni Medina, M.A.Ed., *Managing Editor*
Diana Kenney, M.A.Ed., NBCT, *Content Director*
Dona Herweck Rice, *Series Developer*
Robin Erickson, *Multimedia Designer*
Timothy Bradley, *Illustrator*

Image Credits: p.2-3 iStock; p7. American Institute of Physics/Science Source; p8. Ai Wire/Newscom; p.10 iStock; p15. Turner, Orren Jack/Library of Congress p16. (illustration) Timothy Bradley; p.18 (illustration) Timothy Bradley; p.19 iStock; p.25 Getty Images/Dorling Kindersley; p.26 iStock; p.27 © Blend Images/Alamy; p.28-29 (illustrations) Timothy Bradley; p.31 iStock; p.32 Hemis/Alamy; all other images from Shutterstock.

Library of Congress Cataloging-in-Publication Data
Barchers, Suzanne I. author.

Conservation of energy / Suzanne Barchers.
     pages cm
     Summary: "Rub your hands together. The quicker you move them, the warmer they feel. This is from friction and the movement of energy. Although energy may change forms, it cannot be created or destroyed. But where does the energy go?"-- Provided by publisher.
     Audience: Grades 4 to 6
     Includes index.
     ISBN 978-1-4807-4723-4 (pbk.)
     1. Force and energy--Juvenile literature. I. Title.
     QC73.4.B365 2016
     531.62--dc23
                                            2015002711

Teacher Created Materials

5301 Oceanus Drive
Huntington Beach, CA 92649-1030
http://www.tcmpub.com

ISBN 978-1-4807-4723-4
© 2016 Teacher Created Materials, Inc.

Table of Contents

Energy for the Day

Sunlight peeks through your window early on a Saturday morning. The light and warmth wake you from a deep sleep. You wander lazily down the hallway to the kitchen where you turn on a light and pour a bowl of cereal. You'll definitely need energy for today's big game!

From the sunlight to your steps down the hallway to the cereal you'll quickly eat, energy is everywhere. We cannot see energy, but we can see its effects. When the wind blows a leaf through the air or the sun lights up the sky, energy is involved.

Energy is the ability to do **work**. In other words, energy makes things happen. The wind and the sun have energy. You use energy to move your body and things around you. Your body uses energy from your food to power these movements. You can sometimes feel energy as warmth.

There are rules about how energy behaves. One of those rules states that energy cannot be created or destroyed. This is known as the *law of conservation of energy*, and it is the first law of **thermodynamics**. Energy can change forms and move from place to place, but there is always the same amount of it.

To better understand how energy cannot be created or destroyed, you must know about types of energy and how they are transferred.

The laws of thermodynamics govern how and why energy is transferred.

Potential and Kinetic Energy

Energy can take many forms. But all of these forms fall into two main types: **potential energy** and **kinetic energy**.

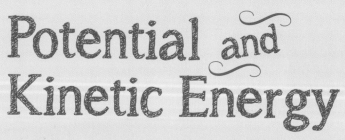

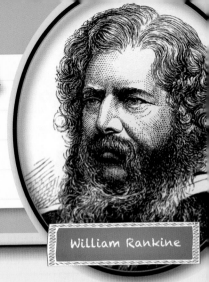

The idea of potential energy has been around since Ancient Greece, when Aristotle began studying the concept. But it wasn't until the 19th century that Scottish scientist William Rankine coined the term *potential energy*.

William Rankine

Potential Energy

Has anyone ever told you that you have potential? This means that you have many possibilities for your future. Potential energy is a similar idea. This is stored energy waiting to be used. Objects with potential energy are not in motion, but they have the potential to move in the future. A roller coaster at the top of a hill has potential energy. Its energy is stored while it is waiting. As the roller coaster begins to fall, it loses potential energy. Energy cannot be created or destroyed. So its potential energy simply turns into moving energy.

There are different types of potential energy. Energy stored by stretching or compressing objects is elastic potential energy. Things such as rubber bands and springs have this type of energy. They have the potential to make objects move.

There is also gravitational potential energy. This is the energy of an object above the ground. As an object falls, it loses gravitational potential energy. This type of energy is affected by an object's **mass**. It is also affected by how high it is above the ground. Things that are heavier or higher above the ground have more of this energy.

Kinetic Energy

Kinetic energy is the energy of motion. Anything that moves has kinetic energy. The kinetic energy of an object depends on its mass. This means that a larger moving object has more energy than a smaller moving object. Kinetic energy also depends on an object's **velocity**, or how fast it's moving. This means that an object moving quickly has more energy than a slower object.

But how do objects get kinetic energy? The law of conservation of energy states that energy cannot be created or destroyed. But energy can move from one place to another. As our roller coaster starts to roll down the hill, its potential energy changes to kinetic energy.

In baseball, some pitchers can throw a ball as fast as 160 kilometers per hour (100 miles per hour). All of that kinetic energy can sometimes shatter the bat!

Measuring Energy

Energy is measured using a few different methods. One unit is the Btu (British thermal unit). One Btu is the amount of **heat** energy it takes to increase the **temperature** of one pound of water by one degree Fahrenheit, at sea level. The joule is named after James Prescott Joule and is the unit for energy in the International System of Measurement. One Btu equals 1,055 joules.

Kinetic energy can also be transferred when objects collide. Take, for example, a game of pool. First, the cue stick hits the cue ball. Kinetic energy transfers from the stick to the ball. Then, the cue ball hits another ball. Kinetic energy transfers from the cue ball to the other ball, making the second ball move.

Energy is all around us. Whether it's stored as potential energy or in motion as kinetic energy, it works.

Forms of Energy

Within these main types of energy, there are specific kinds of energy. These include mechanical, thermal, electrical, and chemical energies.

Mechanical Energy

Objects have **mechanical energy** because of their motion, position, or both. A moving car has mechanical energy because of its motion. A book on a shelf has mechanical energy because it's up high.

Mechanical energy is the sum of kinetic energy and potential energy in an object that is used to do work. Work is done when one object transfers energy to another object. For example, the potential energy from your hand converts to kinetic energy when you swing a hammer. This potential and kinetic energy result in mechanical energy when the hammer collides with the nail, making it move. Work is done.

Every object in motion has mechanical energy.

Thermal Energy

Think about a mug of hot chocolate. The tiny particles that make up the hot chocolate are in motion. The faster they move, the more energy they have. More energy means that they have a higher temperature.

Particles are also in motion in cold objects, but they move much slower. This means they have less energy, which equals a lower temperature.

The total heat energy of all of the particles in a substance is its **thermal energy**. An object's size and temperature affects how much thermal energy it has. A large object usually has more thermal energy than a small one. A warm object usually has more thermal energy than a cool one.

Heating Up to Cool Down

Refrigerators and freezers seem to generate cold, but it is only possible to generate heat! They are actually transferring the faster-moving molecules to a coil attached to the outside of the refrigerator. They are removing heat to cool your food.

Electrical Energy

We use **electrical energy** for many things. We use it to warm and cool our homes. We use it to light our streets and buildings. But we also see it naturally as lightning and static electricity.

Electricity is created when negatively charged particles called **electrons** move between **atoms**. Electrical energy is the flow of this electrical charge.

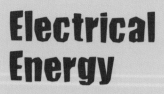

Atoms are so small that they can't be seen with light. Scientists use special microscopes to see them.

proton

neutron

electron

Tiny Particles

Atoms are made up of electrons, protons, and neutrons. Protons and neutrons are in the middle of atoms. But electrons can be free to jump from one atom to another.

Chemical Energy

Chemical energy is a type of potential energy stored in food, fuel, and other matter. Chemical energy can be found in chemical compounds. These are substances made of two or more types of atoms bonded, or joined, together. This energy is stored in their bonds. When these bonds break, new bonds are formed, which release or absorb energy.

Chemical energy is important to life as we know it. In fact, it would be hard to go through the day without it! For example, when we eat, our bodies break down the food and store it as chemical energy. We use this energy to function. This is the same kind of energy stored in gasoline and batteries.

All of these kinds of energy can't be created or destroyed. But they can change and move.

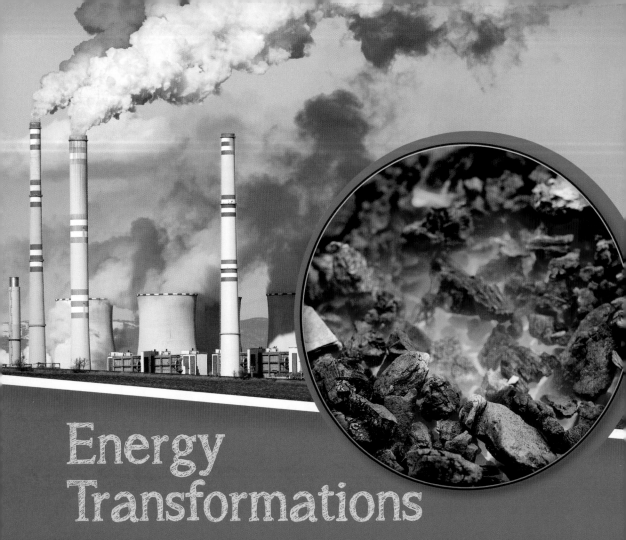

Energy Transformations

Just as the sun's warmth moves through space to warm Earth, energy moves from one place to another. Energy can also go through transformations. This means that energy can change from one form to another. For example, plants turn light energy into chemical energy to make their food. When you stand still, you have potential energy. But when you start to move, it transforms into kinetic energy.

Coal is a source of chemical energy. When coal is burned, its chemical energy transforms into thermal energy. This energy can be used to cook food. It can also be used to turn a generator. This is a machine that transforms thermal energy into mechanical energy. It then transforms mechanical energy into electrical energy to power our homes and cities.

Plants transform the sun's energy into chemical energy through the process of photosynthesis.

Einstein's Theory

Einstein proved that mass and energy are related. He created the famous formula $E = Mc^2$ to explain their relationship. It means that energy equals mass times the speed of light squared. In other words, mass can convert into energy, and energy can convert into mass. The more mass something has, the more energy it contains.

$$E = Mc^2$$

Energy is transformed whenever something moves, jumps, runs, or explodes. Whenever something provides light, breathes, thinks, dances, or does anything, it is because energy is changing from one form to another.

When energy transforms, it may also produce heat. Heat is the movement of thermal energy between two objects. But there are many ways in which heat can move.

Heat

If you've ever burned your hand on a hot pan, then you've certainly felt heat. Heat is the movement of thermal energy and can happen in three ways: conduction, convection, and radiation.

point of contact

point of contact

Conduction

Thermal energy can move from one particle to another. As a molecule heats up, it begins to move. It shakes rapidly and bumps into other molecules. Heat is transferred as the molecules bump. This energy is passed between all of the molecules of an object through direct contact. This transfer is called *conduction*. It continues until all the molecules have the same amount of thermal energy.

Imagine a metal spoon resting on a hot pan. The hot pan is made up of fast-moving molecules. These molecules crash into the slower molecules of the cool spoon. The slower molecules in the spoon begin to move faster and become hotter. The process of conduction is repeated by the spoon. It does not stop until all of the molecules have the same amount of energy.

This is why it feels nice to place your cold hands on a warm mug. The heat from the mug is conducted to your cold hands, making them feel warmer.

Convection

Thermal energy can also move through convection. Convection is the transfer of heat by the rise and fall of heated fluid, such as air or water. This flow of heat is called a *current*. Currents travel in a cycle.

First, heat makes the air or water expand. When air or water expands, it becomes less dense. Material that is less dense always rises above denser material. As the air or water rises, it begins to cool, making it sink down again. Cooler air or water moves in to replace the air or water that rose. And so the cycle continues.

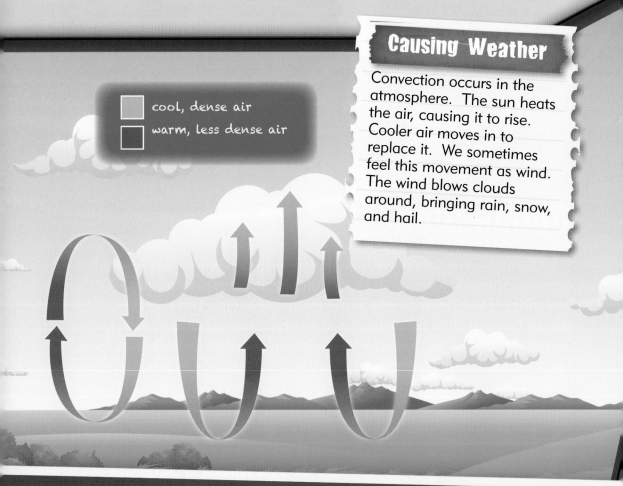

Causing Weather

Convection occurs in the atmosphere. The sun heats the air, causing it to rise. Cooler air moves in to replace it. We sometimes feel this movement as wind. The wind blows clouds around, bringing rain, snow, and hail.

☐ cool, dense air
◼ warm, less dense air

We use convection to cook. Imagine cooking spaghetti on the stove. When you place the spaghetti in a pot of water, the noodles sink. As the temperature from the stove heats the water, the spaghetti rises. The spaghetti is following the rise and fall pattern of the convection currents in the water.

Convection heaters work in a similar way. They start by heating the air around them. As the air warms up, it expands and moves upward. The warm air cools and moves down toward the heater. The heater heats the cool air again, and the cycle continues.

Gases in the atmosphere circulate through convection.

Radiation

Thermal energy can also be transferred through radiation. Radiation is the transfer of heat through electromagnetic waves. These are waves that can move through empty space or matter. These waves do not need molecules around them to move their energy. Of the three methods of heat transfer, radiation is the only one that can do this. Conduction and convection need something for the heat to travel through.

One source that produces electromagnetic radiation is the sun. It comes from extremely hot gases that burn in the sun. It sends this radiation through millions of miles of empty space. We see it in the form of sunlight. When the radiation reaches Earth, it begins to heat the molecules in the sky and in the ground.

Fire also emits radiation. It does this with waves, which transfer heat to objects by radiation. A person near a campfire will feel the radiated heat of the fire. This is true even if the surrounding air is cold. Fire also transfers heat to the surrounding air by convection. This happens as the air around the fire heats and expands.

Without heat transfer, everything would stay the same temperature. Next time you're enjoying a warm meal or the air conditioning on a hot day, you can thank heat transfer.

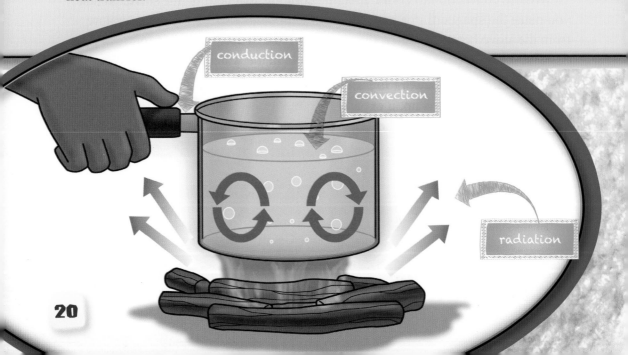

People radiate heat! In fact, any matter that is warmer than the air around it radiates heat.

Heat Around You

Look around you and see if you can find places where heat is being transferred. Is it transferred through conduction, convection, or radiation?

Laws of Thermodynamics

You already learned the first law of thermodynamics. This states that energy cannot be created or destroyed. But it can change form through transformations. The second law of thermodynamics has to do with energy that seems to be lost.

The second law of thermodynamics states that although energy cannot be created or destroyed, some energy may not be used to do work—it is wasted. This concept is known as **entropy**. For example, you may have noticed that a laptop heats up after you have used it for a while. The computer is not using that heat energy to do work. It's wasted heat.

Nothing is perfect. All systems will lose some energy through entropy. In fact, if no new energy is added, a system will eventually run out of energy. Then, it won't be able to do any work.

For example, when you pump the pedals hard on your bike, you can coast for a while. But soon, you begin to lose speed, so you pump the pedals more. If you do not transfer any new energy to the bike, it will eventually stop.

Although entropy can't be avoided, people work hard to try to make things that use energy as efficiently as possible.

Entropy can also be seen when a lightbulb transforms electrical energy to light energy. Not all of the electrical energy becomes light. Some of that energy converts into heat. This is wasted energy if it is not used to produce work in a system. How efficiently, or how well, an object transforms energy is its energy conversion efficiency. An object is highly efficient when it uses most of the energy put into it to do work.

For example, a hammer uses most of the energy from your arm to drive a nail into the wood. The nail, the wood, and the hammer heat up, but not much. A traditional lightbulb, on the other hand, is very inefficient. Most of its energy is turned into heat. This is why it's better to use energy-efficient lightbulbs. They waste less energy.

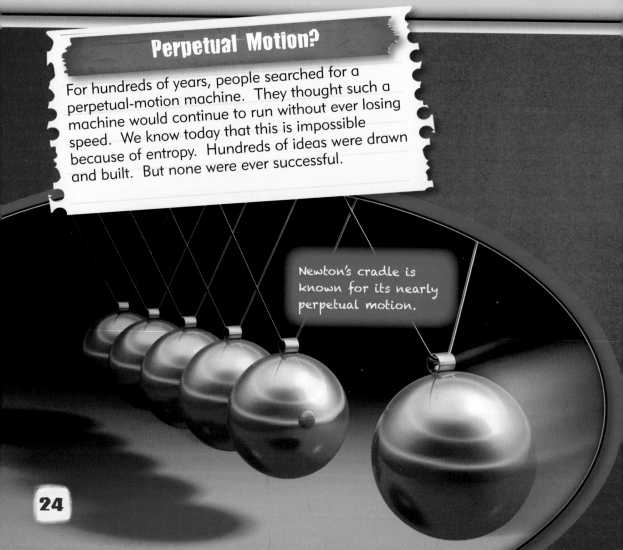

Perpetual Motion?

For hundreds of years, people searched for a perpetual-motion machine. They thought such a machine would continue to run without ever losing speed. We know today that this is impossible because of entropy. Hundreds of ideas were drawn and built. But none were ever successful.

Newton's cradle is known for its nearly perpetual motion.

Engineers are always looking for ways to make things use energy more efficiently. Machines are energy efficient if they can do the same amount of work with less energy. They are also energy efficient if they can do more work with the same amount of energy. Either way, efficiency adds up to energy savings!

The search for perpetual motion dates back to the 12th century.

An inventor attempts to create a perpetual-motion machine.

Energy Is Everywhere

Energy is all around us. Without it, nothing would live, move, or react. Energy literally makes the world go 'round.

Think about all the energy you are using as you read this book. Your heart is pumping blood, and your lungs fill with air. Your body is digesting the food you just ate. Perhaps you are tapping your foot or playing with your hair. All these things require energy. But the law of conservation of energy states that this energy cannot be created—energy always comes from somewhere else. People use the chemical energy from the food they eat. But that energy came from something else. The law also states that energy cannot be destroyed. What work is this energy doing? There is also lost heat through entropy, so our bodies radiate that heat away. Because of this, we must continue to put more energy into our bodies to keep them functioning.

This is just the energy involved in your body, but there are so many other ways we use energy throughout the day. The sun heats the ocean, which causes weather patterns. Electricity is used to power all the appliances in your home. Where else do you see energy? Once you start noticing it, you'll see it everywhere!

Think Like a Scientist

How does an object's height affect its energy?   Experiment and find out!

What to Get

- chair or stool
- meter stick
- rubber ball

What to Do

1 Hold the ball out in front of you about waist high. Let go of the ball, and have a friend measure how high it bounces.

2 Record your results in a chart like this one.

Starting Point	Bounce Height
waist	
shoulder	
above head	
stool or chair	

3 Repeat Step 1, this time holding the ball level with your shoulder. Record the bounce height.

4 Repeat again, holding the ball high above your head. Record the bounce height.

5 Stand on a chair or stool and hold the ball high above your head. Drop the ball and record how high it bounces.

6 Review your chart. How does the ball's height affect how high it bounces? Where did this energy come from?

Glossary

atoms—the smallest particles of a substance that can exist by themselves

chemical energy—energy stored in food, fuel, or other matter

conduction—movement of heat or electricity through something

convection—movement in a gas or liquid in which the warmer parts move up and the colder parts move down

electrical energy—energy produced by a stream of electrons

electrons—negatively charged particles in an atom

entropy—measure of disorder in a system

heat—the movement of thermal energy

kinetic energy—energy possessed by an object due to its motion

mass—the amount of matter an object contains

mechanical energy—the energy objects have because of their motion and position

potential energy—energy possessed by an object due to its position; stored energy

radiation—transfer of heat through empty space by waves

temperature—the average amount of kinetic energy of an object's particles

thermal energy—total energy of all particles in a substance

thermodynamics—study of the movement of heat

transformations—complete or major changes from one form of energy to another

velocity—the rate of change in speed and direction

work—transfer of energy that results from a force moving an object

Index

Circus Act

Carefully observe the picture above. Can you see different forms of energy? Is energy being transferred? Is heat being produced? Name as many different types of energy as you can. Compare your observations with a partner, and discuss any differences.